Praise for *Heaven's Burning Porch*

"If the human relationship to nature is casually brutal and blind to harmony, we should expect little from the relationships humans have with each other. These are the stakes of this haunting and powerful book of poetry, where fear and threat mingle with beauty and love. Add to this mixture the binding agent of religion, and the ingredients for a southern Gothic are in place. But that leaves the possibility of redemption, which if not fully delivered, at least fills the mind of the young protagonist with knowledge and naming, and the prospect of coming through. This book impresses with its careful detail and its unavoidable walk between shame and hope, anguish and affection. The poet offers a hair-curling read, but a sure hand behind the art, and the art, as one would hope, transforms the whole."

—Maurice Manning, author of *Railsplitter*

"In *Heaven's Burning Porch*, James Dunlap writes of a hardscrabble childhood deep in a fever dream of Arkansas where stars burn like 'nibs of bone. . . in a black rag' and ponds fester 'like a cup of water in a charred turtle shell.' The landscape is alive in this book, and often seething, not just a backdrop but a character itself. It is a place laden with inexorable violence, often unleashed by fathers onto sons who 'never talk about the roughhewn hours /spent in the grip of rougher men.' Dunlap's poems have been hammered out at that old crossroads of the brutal and the beautiful. They light up the darkness like a tree 'broke out in a rash of flames.' Read this stunning debut. It will wound you in the best of ways."

—Brian Barker, author of *Vanishing Acts*

The TRP Southern Poetry Breakthrough Series

Series Editor: J. Bruce Fuller

The TRP Southern Poetry Breakthrough Series highlights a debut full-length collection by emerging authors from each state in the southern United States.

Books in this Series:
Arkansas: James Dunlap, *Heaven's Burning Porch*
Florida: Caridad Moro-Gronlier, *Tortillera*
Georgia: Erin Ganaway, *The Waiting Girl*
Texas: Lindsay Illich, *Rile & Heave*
Louisiana: Chris Hannan, *Alluvial Cities*
Mississippi: Noel Polk, *Walking Safari: Or, The Hippo Highway*
North Carolina: Sally Stewart Mohney, *Low Country, High Water*
Tennessee: William Kelley Woolfitt, *Beauty Strip*

Heaven's Burning Porch

POEMS

James Dunlap

The University Press of SHSU
Huntsville, TX

Published by TRP: The University Press of SHSU
Huntsville, Texas 77341
Library of Congress Cataloging-in-Publication Data

Names: Dunlap, James (James William), author.
Title: Heaven's burning porch : poems / James Dunlap.
Other titles: TRP Southern poetry breakthrough series.
Description: Huntsville : Texas Review Press, [2022] | Series: The TRP
Southern poetry breakthrough series
Identifiers: LCCN 2021045677 (print) | LCCN 2021045678 (ebook) | ISBN
9781680032758 (paperback) | ISBN 9781680032765 (ebook)
Subjects: LCSH: Rural families—Arkansas—Poetry. | Arkansas—Poetry. |
LCGFT: Poetry.
Classification: LCC PS3604.U5468 H43 2022 (print) | LCC PS3604.U5468
(ebook) | DDC 811/.6—dc23
LC record available at https://lccn.loc.gov/2021045677
LC ebook record available at https://lccn.loc.gov/2021045678
Author photo courtesy: Carol Dunlap
Photo fragment/reflection: Dave Hoefler @ unsplash
Cover photo and design: PJ Carlisle

Table of Contents

I

A Fable

in the beginning there was a boy and there was a field
in the field the boy shot blackbirds just to see them fall
the boy passed summer bird to bird burr-covered and dizzy
his chigger-bitten legs dangling up in the cracked open sky
and his only friends were a boy with butter-colored hair
that smelled like rain and horses and an old dog so mangy
he looked like an armadillo no one else knew the boy
one day the boy's daddy prayed a shotgun slug into his boy's mouth
and he sat smoldering in the field for two days like a haybale
because the body only knows its own dark appointments
because it wasn't enough to be scared there had to be blood
because the boy thought maybe jesus hated his father too
and now his shattered skull has made for him a strange crown

Primal Forms

Night ascends slow and half-hearted
in its halo of stars. Ticks getting fat
on our blood, the buck moon light
unspooling in the sweet gum's dry leaves.
Pilfered whiskey's bitter twang
like a mouthful of turpentine—half a jug deep
and high-necked, me and Larry Don
out on Thad Williams' land with its ten cows
leaned into one lonely tree. This field
the last refuge from my creeping dreams.
Larry Don looks like a highland steer
rearing his head up under his shaggy hair
and he's got a bundle of bottle rockets
in one back pocket, his daddy's flask in the other.
We have the same bruises, the three ovals
marching down our forearms. We slip
through the barbedwire fence easy,
carrying off shadows of our own.
Our ache blooms nightly, but we tuck it away
and never talk about the roughhewn hours
spent in the grip of rougher men.
Hands that split our brows and black out the sun.
Set loose and drunk we are like our daddies out here.
Too little self-respect to feel shame.
Too dark to see what we're shooting at
but we keep shooting bottle rockets, sending the cows
trundling on their sweat-reeking haunches.
This must be what the old days were like,
cows sending up swarms of drought dust,
no real vision in the field, just primal forms tearing
through the darkness around the lonely dry tree;
their only shelter out here. There's not much saying
what made me do it, but I leveled on the tree and sent
my last bottle rocket straight into the leaves
and it broke out in a rash of flames shining out
like a thick vein of lightning stuck into the field.
In minutes it bristled with black scales, whistling with heat.
The cows dispatched to the far ends of the land,
we watched from the fence as long as we dared, happy
to see their home on fire, something else burning.

and the blade whistles

dark in the field and grandpaw still hacks with a slingblade
he hit grandmaw again and the sky has gone over to a rash
of stars nibs of bone burning in a black rag *and the blade whistles*
every night my stomach sputters like a wet match *and the blade whistles*
grandmaw never cries *and the blade whistles* by now Bud Charton
has quit the haybarn and the tractor's cooling and clicking
and the blade whistles night shucking itself to blackness
and the blade whistles grandmaw learning to do makeup
in a broken mirror *and the blade whistles* grandpaw is a black tongue
bleeding into the field *and the blade whistles* grandmaw churns
out the gravel when she leaves for town *and the blade whistles*
heavy-lidded on the porch I can't move my legs I've hauled brush
until I'm stiff as the boards swelling under me *and the blade whistles*
I'm falling and unfalling asleep *and the blade whistles* I'm floating
over the gumball tree over every snake bed in the county
and the blade whistles the pond like a cup of water in a charred turtle shell
and the blade whistles no, I'm being carried in a sinew-strung arm
nestled like a horsehair on barbwire fence *and the blade whistles*
all I can hear is the buzz of my hornet-nest heart over grandpa's
shoulder *and the blade whistles and the blade whistles*

Unkilling a Deer

For Tiana

the knife saws back along the skin's edge seaming its rent robes

back together the blood crawls back up the groin testicles unhack

blood the frost gives it back up and keeps giving it back up

the dogs spit up chunks of bloody deer heart unsnarling

and their bark comes back in their chest as a rattle and a whimper

the comealong wench cranks back down the hook out the tendon

the antler crown thumps the ground bone crack and my fourteen-

year-old back shoving him through a mudrut back to the truck

flinging him bodily in the bed back down the dirt road

tires popping rocks bringing down the dust daddy's cigarette

unflings itself comes back burning through the cracked window

like a small torch that can't burn bright enough but won't die out

plumes of steam swirl back into my mouth the thick tongue is back

the paleness comes back, the redness leaving like the snags of cloud

breaking themselves over the back of Wolverton mountain

back to the stand the percussive thud melts out of the air echoing

my daddy's grin leaks away that rare that possum grin it's gone

flecks of blood explode back into the deer chest back into the hung skeleton

back into the string of veins gun barrel chokes on its white-hot cough

my finger untrembles lets go of the trigger I bring back the big breath

unclench the gun unload the bullet unclimb the stand bite back the call's grunt

until I'm just a boy walking under a winter-ash sky behind my daddy

saying how the clouds hang like catfish heads on a trotline swinging

JimmyJack's Rain Essay

This dead tree is like a spike or a steeple, a church for the animals. Worms are prophesizing
deep in the season of decay, chanting their religion of rot. Down in the holler, rain

hisses, dimlit in the sweet and mossy air. Even the dead things have their spiritual lives.
I bagged my first thunder chicken when I was twelve. He came struttin and tick-pickin in the rain

and it was hard to see through the woods and the black feathers. His last breath was a pink mist.
Here we bring card tables out on the porch and play dominoes when the angels slosh out the rain.

Grandpa thunders and slams the table with his fist when he throws a five down, *fever up a cat's ass,*
run kitty run. We lose ourselves in a few hours of bones. Everything gets scoured clean in the rain.

April, and the honeysuckle gnaws at the barbedwire like a baby teething on a frozen warshrag.
I like to draw the bead of nectar from them, even though Sissy told me it was snake piss.

Bud Charton lost his arms in a hay baler and god damn if he wasn't on that tractor a few months later.
He told me when it happened, he could see his meat and yellow pearls of fat and when it rains,

he can feel pain running the rail of his ghost-arm, ache clanking all the way up his arm bone.
It's something to see him tearing down the turnrows, spinning that tractor with his nubs in the rain.

About a half mile down Crow's Loop, there's an abandoned bus that's sunk up to its haunches
in mud. Me and Larry Don used to lay up on the seats, calicoed and sun-busted while the rain

leaked and dripped through rusted rivets and cracked windows. The dogwoods in the grove press
their white crosses to the window. Jesus doomed them to smallness. When you nap in the rain

it's hard to know if the world you wake to is real or not. If the moss that sidles down the seams
is the dream greening the world over. You wake up, you're finer than a frog hair split nine ways.

When I was young, about chest high to a mule, a wild hog tore up our corn patch and got hisself
a full belly. Well, we was out of shotgun slugs and he was likely to eat the whole damn patch,

so my daddy caught him in a throw net and put him in the barn to fatten him up and slaughter him.
Momma brought out a bowl of cream corn and lard and a five-gallon bucket full of rainwater.

My daddy said *listen, boy. Don't close that lock, I caint find the key to that sumbitch,* pulled the chain
around the door. I'll be damned if I didn't lock it. Lord, my stomach ate itself all night long.

When I told him, he grabbed a hammer and came across the yard, broke the lock off with a single
swing, dropped the hammer, razzed my hair, and walked off. Best time to go catfishing is after rain.

We used to climb the trees on the back acre that were gnawed bare and strung with dozens of silk
hammocks. We'd use cane poles to whack every live nest and them old baltalkie worms'd rain

down by the handfuls. My grandpa showed me how to bite their heads off and sleeve them down
the hook inside out. Catfish love the worms. Them worms eat and green shit; eat and green shit.

Now, I'm sure one day the lord will call down my sins, but for tonight rain
is thumping and ringing on every tin roof in the county, summer's reign

is still burning through the last whip of sunlight over Wolverton mountain,
and the river's high and by god almighty there's catfish in the skillet and a sleepy dog licking

meat scraps off my boots and I ain't never seen anything better than rain
come warshing down the mountain in sheets like pearl skinned church ladies joined at the arm.

The Dark Herd

Four hours sunk under a fever festering in the swollen ropes of my brain.
Sweat print in the bed. I dreamed an angel into the corner, retching a red camber.
        Spitting image of my daddy.
                Heat enough to drive me out of my own body.

Gravel rattle and the guttering bur of his pick-up.
Momma galling him for being out all night. I walk out to see
a poached button buck frostbitten in the truck bed, chest peppered open
with buckshot, the head nearly hacked off.

Daddy razzes my hair too hard and he smells like corn cobs and gin,
puts up his calloused palms for me to punch. He grabs me up and heaves me
over his shoulder like a stringer of dead rabbits.
                I tell him I'm going to hurt him one day.
        You dreamin boy. I'll beat your head soft.

He staggers a little when he goes to fetch a comealong winch
and his deer skinner, comes back shirtless in a swirl of cigarette smoke.
I take off my shirt too. The cold in me feels like a bullet mushrooming through bone.

I'm sweating. I'm in the way. I'm always in the way.

He shoves me a last time and I go end over end dizzy into a tree.
Everything spinning. Everything lit and hazy through fits of sleet.

I shake the cotton from my head and stay outside. Taste blood.
Persimmons are shining like teeth in the dark. Dried, harder than rocks
when I rack them through the trees with a sawmill slab
                    and hear their distant thump come back.
Through the woods and bitter blackness, the moonlight sluices
down the treeline in white hemorrhages like tattered magnolia blooms.

In the sweet coldness of the wind, my arms blue as catfish bellies,
I remember the pine slab I'm white-knuckling, splinters biting into my hands.
        Daddy if you had any teeth left, I'd send them spinning clean
             out of your rot-softened jaw. Every boy I've ever hit
             has carried off the beating I've owed you.

But I am the weakest person I know—
                only and always attending to this dark herd gathering in my chest.

Night Fishing

I'm back to the oldest forms: time and darkness.
The boat knocking   in a crow-black lake, moon
like a bleached turtle shell, fog nuzzling our hands.
My father   fishes point, easing us along the bank
under the gnarled backs of lake-trees, his spotlight flickering
waterline to tree-line   —spiders falling   from their wires of light
a cottonmouth   yawning on a branch,   its reeking mouth
dishinged   as if he was eating what's left of the night.
My father believes pain is the best teacher: the rusty whistle
of the yo-yo   tripped too early, he throws the oil-gummed pliers
to snap the hook shank from my fist, my hand, this crippled
fish bleeding   from its mouth.   There is something blooming
and swelling   like a bed of catfish   in all that quiet.
He has always said he's dead, that his bones just haven't rotted yet.
So I imagine my father as an old church piano, all rotten legs and splayed keys,
but here,   I only have a mind of water and he is still rotten
rotten   like the cracked open mouth   of a dead gar—
each curved tooth a shard of yanked starlight.

II

A Good Year for Pecans

—Central Arkansas, April

The plum trees are wearing their crowns of thorn again
and the clouds that hang like shreds of dried tobacco
are sliding away like clots of oil in an empty lake—
the persimmon tree, dying in a nest of its own fruit,
now ripped in half, now yanked out of socket,
its roots like thorns pulled from a muddy paw, no sound
but the green whisper of pine needles raining down
from the single tree left standing, and I haven't seen
enough of this night to know what it means
that the sickle blade moon shudders and scratches
out with its tine the hours of no electricity,
the hours of shrieking branches, the haze of gasoline,
the ripping teeth of chainsaws, scratches out the story of a land
that mile after mile, has gone down to flood and fire.

＊

Some years summer gets here in a hurry, as if heat
were something driven by galloping horses
and everyone is tense and strung tight—
                              they know it's easy to make a storm—

so easy to walk outside after a week of no rain and come back up
a dozen days later hip-deep in flood water and swollen boards,
chickens roosting in a tree like flying birds do.

Evening and the horses stand blinking in their own shadows,
swaying on their hooves like lazy leaves,
                              picking at the curls of dried dirt

like ochre fish scales, their tails swatting the last few flies
from their sweat-frothed flanks and the rabbits, they sleep deeply

in heat like this—the barn shakes and swims in my vision,
                              even the pokesalad
hangs its head, as if to shake the heat from its dreaming head.

Only April and every creature in the county is hurting for water,
                              is shuffling on however many feet to even a snag of shade.

It started in the orchard, the apples, riven with heat, bobbing in halos of flies,
it started in the fanged brush around the pond, now raked to a muddy fist,
the wind started whistling through the ditches and the swirled flutes of haybales.

The sky broke into shapes I don't know—the color of dead lichen.
Then the siren's long black moan like a high up haint.

Then everything happened.
                              And we let it happen:
cicadas and funnel clouds, fig-sized hail and cricket baskets
tumbling through the thin grass. And we let the roof tear off
and fly across the yard, over ash-colored hills, wind-stripped trees,
                              a rusted metal bird with a god-sharp vision.

12

*

Some have walked many miles on legs heavy as rebar,
                                        stiff with dread,
just to pluck a doll eye from a two-by-four
or to find their dog still chained to a tree,
                            the collar so deep in the blackening neck
the head is hanging
                        only by the wires of veins and a twig of spine,
the body is bent to running
like its days spent in puppy dreams under the porch,
                            its opened skull a chamber for the music of flies.

They have walked the miles of splintered poles
and their fallen black tendrils to see the empty yawn of a broken tree,

their houses bearing their strange crosses of trees splintered across their backs
slinging their shadows over everything that can be touched.

Who can blame the man for punching the chickencoop,
                                        the only thing he has left?
Its metal smack like someone above us nailing the lid shut.
No one stops him even when the bones crack and jostle in their sockets.

They know they can't stop this.

Everyone looks away: the man breaks himself on a chicken house full of drowned birds.
He's moved to breaking the wood and chickenwire with his heel.

His wife, still in her nightgown touches his shoulder, says, *Bill, please.*

There's not enough light left to do any good.
        Spotlights swinging through the woods of busted branches.
                                        Hounds bay. Horses chuff. Cows
bawl.

They can't so much see the dark as feel it.
                    And they must feel the growing dark is not just from the outside.

*

I lay sweating in bed, moonlight washing my room.
Down the hall, I hear Don Williams singing *nothing makes a sound in the night like wind does.*
I get up and walk outside past my daddy in his chair snoring, tobacco spit running down his chin.

Out in the leftover wind, the laconic pond swelled
and gloving the okra stalks that curl silently into the dark like the fingertips of the dead.
Treeshadow. The wind is picking up again and the magnolias are knocking elbows. I remember
the rest of that song: *but you ain't afraid if you're washed in the blood like I was.*

＊

Every night I fell into the blackest soil, washed in from the river,
                              kinking into mud like a tadpole chest down in a creek.

That first step off the porch, silt and leaves, a length of barbedwire
hanging from the hickory tree, every question I have never asked
                              smeared its reeking breath over the house,

over the unbroken rock work, the pumphouse bowed and swelling
in the humidity, the screen door, softly, with the rasp of wind and flies.

Morning and I walked that snapped spine of land and its myriad climates:
one patch dry and crumbling another sunk under oil-heavy water.

I came to a field of pines. Centuries old.
            Dozens of them laying in each other's arms and the many left standing
in various forms of reproach. I play, like any other day,

over and through the ochre crosshatch of limbs, throwing pinecones.

Who knows what I was looking for,
but I found a litter of raccoons trembling in a nest of busted branches

and their eyes still burn, half-buried in my rusted guts like an unripe apple.
                              I knew something of their hunger.

How high is the water papa

it's come a long way to knock down the fishhouse

How high is the water momma

*they ain't any field left anymore the rocks and the bugs
and the creatures can't sang no more*

How high is the water papa

*the fridge pump is chugging up water, the bacon's
gone rotted and the bread's as black as a deer tick's back*

How high is the water momma

*our house is an alter to mosquitoes and snakes blessed
with water—the bullfrogs blessed with a little more
water*

How high is the water papa

*hand me that hammer—the ball peen—I gotta break the
roof open—all that water and all the heat in one shack—
this leaking place is riven with flies*

How high is the water momma

*yesterday I saw a bowlegged dog floating on a door
just staring at his own mutt face in the water*

How high is the water papa

*I saw a muskrat the size of a baby bear in the ditch the
other day. I hope to hell the water ain't reached the cornpatch*

Pecans on the roadside, pecans in the ditch.
Hunched backs up and down the blue-chip spine
of Highway 9, with their granny bead necks and torn shirts.
Before the storm every pecan tree down by the lake
was full of little brown eyes.
It was a big hand that shook them down.
Now everybody that can is dragging burlap sacks
burdened with mud and pecans.

*

God has put his fist down on us

Someone shut off the sound this morning and silence crept on filthy paw over every gravel road once clogged with a haybaler's bowed tines catching and tearing honeysuckle vines and saw briars. I miss the blistered cough of a flatbed diesel filling with gravel and Steve Crow calling someone useless as tits on a bull, and I miss blueticks baying with the church bell that rings every morning except this morning. Even the banty, handsome boy, wouldn't pick his head up this morning. The sky sags over every broken tree and twisted fence. The church is nothing but a chimney now and a spine and the bell is in a tree and some raccoon had a mind to make it his home. I can't help but grow so thin, when I see it all, that I'm lost like a snag of power line in a hayfield without borders and I wonder if god can look on all this ruin and not turn away, take off his hat—maybe his face is as blank as momma's when she hangs up clothes, her hands strung with that same onion-peel skin her momma has. Today, when she sings *When I die, hallelujah by and by, I'll fly away*, I believe it, maybe for the first time.

*

I wonder why we don't name our tornadoes.
                              That night we had seven—
I would call them the Pleiades, those bone-tired sisters who've run
their sandals to pieces,
                              picking their way over the minnow-light of the moon
dissolving in the spillway, through the old and thick grasses
                                        in the old no-name cemetery by the lake.

Orion born of Dread and Sea, like most of our dads
rises late, spins lazy and drunken
                              over the black-washed hills
hunting women
            over the watertower
and down by the moss-dressed pumphouse,
                              his dogs blood-shod and slavering.

I believe they looked down over a land full
                        of hunters and women-chasers
and evened the score,
                        destroyed their simple second-hand lives.
They broke their trees and drowned their dogs.

＊

Dogs winnow their way through a path of bloody rags,
crusty patches of insulation, strips of treebark, hanks of bloody animals
                                        churning with flies.
There wasn't much flood in the highland, just cracked and cratered heads
from hail about the size of a pig's brain—beyond that,
no one could say Birdtown changed.
                Same milo bobbing in the field, same gouts of light sprent over the lake.

Bud Miller's place is humming
                with police pickups and field nurses.
No one lives out there anymore. No one save Bud and half a dozen hunting dogs
that don't hunt anymore. Bud, they say has a cold gizzard instead of a heart—
he once hit his wife with a brick over a burnt pan of cornbread.
Their marriage was one long knock-down-drag-out.

She's left now. Back to her momma. Doing better.

His house reeks like horse-mud and he don't care,
his clothes are dissolving off his back—
                it's awful hard for anyone to shake the man's hand
even when he gets to town for a case of beer and some cans of potted meat.

He was out mowing when they hit
                and now he sits cross-legged on a tailgate, his feet dangling like a child's,

a nurse leaching blades of grass from his skin,
                each about three inches long, each bloodslick and trembling—

his face as blank as a stubblefield until he sees his horse broken against a tree,
its open chest an organ loft blooming with maggots,

ribs like doubled over oaks, her braided hair crusted down her back.
The nurse watches the grass blades sliding out of his skin like thin bloody fish.

No one here likes to see a man cry.

*

I'm out in the backcountry again on the dirtroads washed off,
caked smooth with Arkansas mud.
                    Bloated ditches on each side.
I ease along, my tires biting and slinging, couple bobbers clanking
on the end of fishing poles. I shouldn't be surprised how different it all looks.
                                        And I'm not.
Even a hawk on a stump is strange, like a bad taxidermy job.

Right church, but the wrong pew.

I stop for a snapper turtle sunk desperately in the road's mud
and I think he wants to fight. He hisses and shows me his mouth, a reeking pouch,
furred with algae.
                    He pushes hard to make his own way
out of the sippyhole. He'd rather die crossing than owe me anything.

Back in the truck. Back down the mud road past the gas station
with a box out front my cousins said was full of snakes.

The road is long and I get caught remembering my nightmares.
For many nights I had a dream of the end of these simple things.
It always starts with ash and fades into water and somewhere in between there's wind.
                    All things end in the river.

In the dream, after the ash, I walked for five days across Overcup,
down Highway 9, and up Petit Jean mountain,
and I climbed to the top of a boulder in Bear Hollow
and the treeline looked like possum teeth in that wasted jaw plate of land.
I looked out over the land and the river was choked with thorns and rimmed in fire.

I come back to myself in the truck in enough time to turn down Rural Route 551
towards Brewer Lake. And there's a place in the hills, down a pigtrail,
where you can see most of Overcup, so I back in and get up on roof of the truck.

I see the land with my real eyes: chicken houses, barges in the river.
And mile after mile of fresh lumber tilting in morning's first spit light.

III

Peanut's Catfish Essay

Nailed to the fence plank after plank, skinned catfish going for forty cents
a pound if you can find them. Too-hot summer and thin catfish.

Dogs pick through piles of skin and fat-veined innards. Peanut just keeps fileting.
He's worked himself raw. His shop is hung with drying rabbit skins, not just catfish.

These days pig ears and horse teeth. Barrels of guts he calls *flysweets*. He makes money
on channel cat bellies, but he loves stuffing bears and deer heads. Ain't had a hundred in catfish

money cross his hands this summer and that was for spoonbill. They make jerky bait of it,
you smell it all night down the holler. Strips so rank they'll knock a dog off a gut-wagon. Catfish

Bufford had a dog that ate hisself dead on beef guts. His stomach broke open and spilled out like wet
circus peanuts. He takes himself to the clapboard church on Pigpin road. Eats a mess of fried catfish.

Dances and dances. The porch bows under his clodhoppers. He smells like grass and guts.
His overalls riot with flies. The tin roof shakes rattles loose flakes of rust. His freezer is empty of catfish.

Such a rotten summer. He can't love a woman. He can't catch fish.
But he can dance if there's a fiddle tune and a whiskey jug. At night he dreams of catfish.

He dreams he is the hand ripping them from their beds in hollow logs up and down the river
like strung out blue tremors. He closes his eyes to a world of whiskers and and mud.

Elegy

For Josh

There is so little light left in the field. April rain
rubbing its velvet antlers on the windowscreen,

wind in the trees like the rasp of a hog's punctured lung,
fog over the ground like a herd of talcumed horses.

Nearly a year since you came to your reward
and it's hard to believe anything good ever happened here.

I'm dressing fish in the rain.
Scales clot in the sugarspoon, scales sprent like birdshot.

I'm sure you've cleaned fish this way too:
split him from asshole to brisket, take the head and the guts come with it.

You know everything I know—the dead always do.
We know a fish is a nimbus in the pond's darkness, a fish is half light, half stone.

We know the hogs, hungry boys like they are,
love the fish, now unburdened of guts, now lightshocked and quievering.

I have half a mind to stay here all evening leaned on this fence
like a busted wagonwheel, watching the night get chained up in lightning.

Maybe I have it wrong.
Maybe the body's greatest gift is the lungs no longer have to swell

and the heart silences into a pulp of its own making.
It can be a gift that the body no longer picks itself up just one more time.

The electric fence clicks:
that's the dead counting stars.

How can I say I only want you to come home?
That I was always afraid when you were?

Boy

It started by the hickory tree in a hollow log that for months
                           has been humming and swelling with yellowjackets.

Late evening, wrecked halos of gnats twisting in the last light.
My daddy shirtless and lean in the grass carrying two cinderblocks
                                   plugs each end of the log,
shakes out a rust jug of gas on it, strikes a match
with his front tooth, then another two and it's all flames and smoke,

his face flecked with yellowjackets mean and dying
and he's grinning to watch something break apart,
                        his teeth like splinters of burnt glass.

✳

Morning, spider-light spinning in the branches.
The cedars out by the hog pen are ready to bust open with ticks.

I'm in the sty slopping, slapping the backs of our hogs,
                        taking a hog's joy in the mud and stink.
Sometimes I think my daddy doesn't know joy
and doesn't understand why I think my body is made of chickenwire
                           because it bows but doesn't break.
He's got another fire going—
               he's always burning something.

＊

The fire is sucking its teeth and huffing the yard a strange black.
He takes my rocking horse behind the ears
                            like when you groom one,
hip-slings it deep in the fire,
                            now big-shouldered and long-fingered
and I can't stop staring at the melted paint dripping and hissing
and the yard smells like it always does: burnt cedar, leaf-smoke, gas.

I can't stop it now, ash-heavy smoke clotting in my mouth,
                   I can't stop, even if I grind this poultice of dust into my tongue,
something like a prayer
                or maybe the shadow of a prayer.
Daddy says he'll give me something to cry about,
                                I'm supposed to be a man now.
Put your fucking hands on a shovel, boy—use that son of a bitch.

＊

Who's to say I'm not still there in the mud squelch and the fangs of sumac
          in the horse chuffs and scorched dirt, in the burnpit and scabby logs,
                                   the thorns and bullet casings?
I'm still there and I'm just a boy.
          And I think I will always be a boy.
The night of my birth my grandfather christened me *boy*
                             and never spoke my name again.
It seems that I came by it honestly, this thread of winnowing light in me.

Beatrice and Cloy's Essay of Night

Every year the cemetery creeps a little closer and one day it will be backed up into the yard.
They were happy. Morning light through the window. When they was married, Cloy drank all night

and all next morning. Lord, he even puked in the collection plate at Second Baptist Church.
Maybe it was all he had to offer God besides his strangled, *Oh Lord of light, Lord of night,*

a tune his momma sang to him in the crib. In the raw stage lights he thought he saw her,
hanging clothes out on the line at the old house. Would his name be in the book under Knight?

Maybe he spent too many years stuck in the muddy roads between doubt and bent knees,
but when he was a kid, he knew the rules: keep out of God's crosshairs; hands to yourself at night.

In the ringing of his cast-iron head, he thought: let my wheezy prayer make it up in the weather.
Beatrice was queen of the dancehall, churn up the saw dust, drink the boys under the table all night.

She still fried chicken every Sunday morning. But now the hitch in her hip galls her every day,
and sweat glitters like fish scales on her forehead. But she ain't the quitting kind, in the long night

of her life, she never asked for a handout. Damn proud of it too. Cloy believed he'd worked
long enough to have some fun. Beatrice had a distaste for fishing and never would swim. One night

she told Cloy when he was chest-deep in the lake, *if you seen as many bodies pulled out of the water
as I have, you wouldn't swim neither. Not on the hottest sumbitchin day, much less at night.*

To Cloy, she never did anything but shine like a five-dollar lure. He always remembered her barefoot,
pregnant in his yard asking for gas money, saying his dually looks like a cat in heat.

Cloy didn't know she smoked in the bars and out in the shed, leaned between ricks of firewood
and hanks of hog-casing strung up like Christmas lights. And each Sunday she prayed a little less.

They never made a fuss at the house anymore. Even when Cloy came to his reward after a catfish
dinner. They was settling in like they did. Her wood whittling, him with his rat killing. Nights
,
like that made Cloy grin like an old mule chewing briars. The pines all jeweled up in stars, wind
settling in the garden. *God hisself never laid a better patch of tomatoes on this whole damn earth.*

He fell asleep on the porch and never woke up. The sheriff hauled his body to town that night,
saw her whittling on the porch, asked what she was making. *I'm making crosses. Beautiful crosses.*

Night of Effigies

Night of Leonids. Sparks in the dark. Night of sky shedding its cinders.
Hills like heaps of ash, and I'm just a lanky boy lost on my own land, the back acres
I'm banned from. This fishing pole over one shoulder, a stringer of catfish
over the other, I cast my eyes into the waters above me, hoping for rain
to break the heat. I've lived my whole afraid my daddy's shortcoming
are somewhere pumping through my own blood. The empty, impotent rage,
the brain fever—I want to shake loose of it. Momma said shooting stars
were pieces of heaven's burning porch crumbling and falling to earth.
I've spent years sick and wanting to leave. One winter, I ran as far as Possum Trot Road.
Seven miles in winter, seven miles of gravel and mud. That night,
I was so hungry for what I left behind, a warm fire, dog named Bandy,
the shape of the words my momma said, I laid nested in the drawn roots
of a fatbottomed oak like a chick ensconced in egg. The snow fell hushed
for miles around me. When sleep finally took me, I dreamt all night of bats,
gnashing teeth and translucent skin black and glistening—
a thousand ink-dipped effigies of night retched forth from the bowels of some cave,
screeching and cutting like bucksaws along the shattered tree line.

Rufus and Ella's Essay of Days

Ella early in the school kitchen. Peel a few potatoes, take a pull from her tin bottle. Take a pull pass it around. 9am and wine teeth. 9am and sciatica lacing her leg in dull pain. Hardest work of the day

still to come. The light skinned women called her Ella Blue cause she so dark and her voice is sad and slow like smoked honey, but when she laughs every pot rings and jangles. Too many days

she's made the fifteen-mile drive, her jeep like a beetle through the grey flake fog. When she saw the new girl, 16, a redhead to boot, she hollered *red on the head and fire in the hole!* So many days

leaves her man ripping bark in bed, worn slick from last night's sweat and tussle. She misses the early days. Her loving like good food: high pressure; high pleasure. She met Rufus on RR 639.

He was dodging truck scales. She was sitting on a butane tank like a searing silver horse. Saturday nights the moon rose out of the scrubpines like a lit bullfrog eye and he'd sling her over his shoulder

in the barbeque line at Wango's. Some years back he took her to the Piggly Wiggly grand opening and they had a seven-pound lobster that walked around on the sales floor like a dog. She loves

him like a burning wagon. She'd go down to hell and yank the devil's tail for him, but hates people knowing it, so at work she yells *God almighty send me a man, I'm done tired of that boy* every day.

Rufus, he's a simple man raised on biscuits and a busted Bible, but tried to understand her appetites. The whiskey at night, the wine early in the day.

Smoking and cussing. *Lord knows what I'm doin* she said once gone for three days. He shrugs and gets back to work welding. His shed is clean save for the slag and rust on the floor, daylight

noodling in through the corners. He has a meat saw from when he failed being a butcher. An old Biro. On hot days he would sit down in the creek and watch minnows nibble dead skin off his hands

and he loved the cedar smells and how they dipped in the breeze. More than anything, Rufus loved owning things. John Deer he won in a hand of poker a pint deep in a jar of juniper moonshine, day-

light shedding its skin over Wolverton Mountain. His Cadillac slicker than greased owl shit with Turtle Wax. He told Ella on his knees one night by the swing, gnats going wild,

tagging her sweet shining skin, *Now Ella Blue, I'm gonna give you a house. No more this trailer shit, you hear me?* Most Sundays, she was slept, her man in the front pew praying for her every day.

And it came to pass that on a Sunday when the wind cut every cloud into dumplings and whistled through every crack in the Second Baptist church, bringing down honeysuckle and smoke, daylight

and hellfire. By God, can you believe a pan of frying chicken could burn a trailer down to the cinderblocks? Rufus in the front pew. Ella still not home from her poker game the night before.

Can you believe a day broke open with smoke? The whole town ended up out there at his place watching them put out the fire. The sheriff toed the burnt dirt and said, *well the lord gives,*

but the devil plays for keeps. Hours later, daylight all spooled out when they finally finished. Rufus knew he was headed for the insurance company next morning, then the bank, then he was going to

start building a home for Ella Blue, who sat on the hood of her jeep wiping her face saying: *The days, lord, the days keep piling up.* That night they slept on her momma's porch, drinking long

into the night, when the mind gets hazy but the body is a live wire.

My horses darkly in the barn

the lights, stars in a mud puddle,
grief of being whole cloistered
in a field. Horses carry their pain
in their bellies, snuffling all night
in bristling heat quick to turn
a body to salt and splay ribs
like heat-riven keys on a piano.
Sometimes I think winter's broken me
as broken as Grandpaw three days
braindead because Grandmaw said
Jesus rose the third day. *Get used
to the heat, life ain't short enough*.
A boy I knew when I was boy just died.
He was so in love with being alone.
He took pills and he took whiskey
and the pills got him first. He took pills
because they sent him to sweet dreams
of his barefoot mamma humming gospels
over a bacon skillet. He came to his reward
cold in the woods, snow under his boots
must have sounded like salt-scrubbing
a kettle as he stomped deeper, swerving
endlessly through leashes of sleet
like a bait-shy fish.

IV

We all Live Leaner More or Less

It's all night burning endlessly, not a dry sheet in the county—
                           this hangdog heat between rain and drought.
Grandpaw never had an air conditioner, so I spend most nights in turns
sleeping and sweating and staring out over the skull-colored bulbs in the cotton patch,
listening to the crickets cranking their music box legs through the Arkansas dark.

Grandpaw's house is dank and musky as the frothed flanks of a stud horse.
Sometimes he would snatch me from my daydreams,
barefoot in the haybarn spun with sun-drunk spiders run out on their crystal stems,
wedged between bales, breathing slowly, working my sinuses raw,
                               his hand was the curl of dusty sunlight
on the scruff of my neck, yanking me up like a bad dog.
Some days he was drunk and sprawling across the tick-swollen yard
                           bur-tagged and hollering
until dark, when he would fall to an ether black sleep on the porch.

❋

My whole summer spent slaughtering rabbits.
I'm cradling the body, bending the legs under the breast, stilling the trembling,

his hands gripping mine using them like they're his own,
he pushes my thumb in the hollow under the skull and over the neck.

Yank his neck, I can smell Copenhagen reeking from the gaps in his teeth
you'll feel it pop and it won't jerk anymore

his hands are bruising mine as he squeezes *do it now while he ain't fightin*
the pops happen, the nausea like a stomach full of minnows

and the sun gets under my skull and seethes in my eye sockets
and my face is wet *that's the hard part, boy* before another breath,

grandpaw has taken the head off and thrown it to the weeds for the slavering dogs.
The rabbit is hanging from strings by the ankles and I'm peeling back the skin—

the guts ease out on their piebald chords
and I'm gagging hard until my chest aches, my nose hairs stitched with the sweet rot

of half-digested pellets *keep one eye on the skillet and one eye on the rabbit*.
Now the skinned form is twisting in the wind like a flesh-wing pendulum

and my nails will be red for the rest of summer and I've never been so happy
to see the lit tips of my fingers sharp in the hottest days of the year.

✳

He taught me how to discern the rising grey flake of a deer panting in a hiss of sleet,
to tuck my jug of driving-whiskey deep in my seat and my dip deep in my cheek
and spit between my boots and shrug off anything. Grandpaw
taught me that is there is no help and no help needed—
                    don't wait to see my empty hand.

I don't trust you, I don't trust you, grandpaw
taught me the persuasiveness of the back of a hand,
                how knuckles are harder than anyone expects.

A prayer is no good if you beg
                a man that live on his knees will die on his knees
and when you have to die pray to god you die in the night,
                    pray to god nobody sees it.

✳

Three years dead and still his hands. Still: his nails like little peeled acorns,
how they gripped my ribcage, lifting me over a nest of thorns to pick a plum.
                The scattered macula on his onion-peel skin.

It's always night when I remember him when shadows come creeping
around like a high-shouldered cat and all I remember is how mean he got.
How he threw a fit and smashed all the mirrors in the house
when grandmaw teased him red for a cowlick.
When he forgot his medicine, he'd yell the roof off the place
and he'd pace and root around banging his fist into the table,
and everything was *horseshit*, and *goddamn that makes my ass wanna suck sour milk.*

My grandpaw living the life of tick:
                    shuffle and bite, shuffle and bite.

37

Front Porch Picking: 2 am: Summer

The wind, the night, falling away star-threaded, in bone-fanged fields.
Childhood porch, childhood sorrows to attend with.
Bats trawling through bottomless dark, stitching the twilight with wires of blind noise.
I'm here for the inventory of my sickly estate: the heat-killed pig in the back sty,
his head split to the thrapple rotting to clusters of shining blackberries,
his head a hive for bees picking his tongue clean sweetly, crystal strands
of drying maggots braided down the rainwater light of not-yet-morning.
The dogwood is strung with dog collars, like macabre windchimes,
Everything here is sick with giving up. I feel it like fat swelling in marrow.
Forgive me my unclean spirit. Forgive my muddy robes.
Sometimes it catches up with me, this fear that I've lived long enough
to become the wasted light that stalks my evenings. I've had my fill
and it has filled me with sparks, and with nothing. Tonight, someone from the county
came and sets fire to the ditches to clear them out. All night threads of flame,
thousands of eyes, smoke dragging its chains up and down the hills,
bull frogs lighting the holler with the sound of a guttering Mack truck.

Miss Darlene's Essay on Light

Miss Darlene trundles like a bowlegged beeve, swinging a bucket of chicken bones and corn cobs.
Them hogs'll tap dance for a mouthful of that shit, mud crusted, they grunt and light

through clots of flies. She can't help smiling even if her knee aches. Plenty of morning left
and too much work for one body. For a bent one with a waterlogged knee. The slop ain't light

but her handsome boys are happy, romping to the stiff twang of the electric fence clicking.
Fat braided into every muscle, pink bridled and swelling with swampy summer light.

The shed full of homefixed baits and deer bones, full of greasy chains and rust-gnawed shovels.
Smell of castor oil and sweet anny. Smell of they-ain't-much-telling hiding there in the light.

She has to sit down more these days, the ice has its way of whittling her bones down thin,
and she wishes she was in a summer, by a creek with a catfish peeling drag on her pole's light

reel. Hungry cows bawling all morning—*Lord, pull your ear down to hear to all this racket?*
Even geese fetching themselves home feels every Sunday washing the hills with cold blue light.

She can't say she's rightly married, but she thinks she was married by a barefooted Baptist, but the boy
runned off somewhere. *Went to take a shit and the hogs ate him.* She lights a fire, she lights

a stogie, shaking with the cold. Even after sweating through yards of pig waste and ice-laced mud,
her pulse thin and thready. Her fingers, their jag-legged dance—skinned minnows in scalded light.

That night, a tooth of moonlight growing long in the window, silence enough to hear spoonchimes
in the clots of darkness flaked with sleet hissing through the trees and caught writhing in the light

of a work barn. She's a pale candle waxed to her bootheel of land, waiting for someone to huff the light
out. Miss Darlene, child of god, caught in his bad eye, filmy with a storm of cataracts.

Giving Thanks

Grandma always said to rub the wound
with the belly of the catfish that horned you,
so I'm back home hiding in the rungs of light
climbing the down empty living room.
Outside, they're frying a bird, his legs upward
as if he jumped in the pot himself. It sounds
like a boiler overheating. They're getting drunk
as a Saturday night dance in the barn downtown,
the floor danced to a poultice of beer and henbit.
I try to fix my face, be happy like them. Two hours south
of here they drop turkeys out of helicopters
and the kids love it. They stomp in the mosaic
of blood and feathers and chase the few survivors.
I keep having a dream where I stand in a field
with a tree full of goat eyes run out on strings
drying and in a hole near a creek there's a baby
covered in hay and bawling. The baby is supposed
to be me, but when I reach for me, the hole is empty
save for some leaves and water. It's like that sometimes,
that what you reach for is already gone, been gone.
And I can't hide anymore, it's all waiting for me,
all I haven't become yet, just out the windowscreen.

Momma's Essay on Faith

She would have been an A-1 sawbones on a wagontrail. The times she's splinted a broke leg
or wrapped a water-fattened ankle in a bandage or yanked a tooth with pliers, placing faith

in a bunch of farm hands to not make a fuss, she fixed up every broken boy in the county. She never
wanted it, she likes the sunshine and quiet. That's all she prayed for. A nurse by trade, but has faith

she'll come to her reward of sunlight and smoked meats and her sweet puppies in the fields. Nights
she spends pouring gummy coffee, giving pain medicine to old men gnashing their gums, faith-

full in their own minds. It's just a smile, a wink. Just a light brush against her perfumed skin. And
she'd give them a few tries for an IV or drop a clipboard on their nuts. It takes some kind of faith

to live out here, to step off the porch in fog so thick you can lay a spoon on it, to walk quiet through
the dark and stumble on a possum's squinty-eyed rage or to stand ankle deep in a frosted morning

in the sty and look out over of a field of black-eyed hogs, in the congress of their slate blue breath,
shake out gallons of slop. My daddy was out sliding and flinging down a shale hill. Shooting rabbits

by spotlight when momma first told me thunder was god smacking mosquitos on his knee.
She'd got me down off the top of the fridge, *my little climbing boy, my shithead*. Her friend Faith

thought I was slow cause there was something funny about the way I talked. They didn't speak
again until Uncle Larry died. Momma kept the fact that the night before he came to his reward, faith

was on his mind. He'd been reading the Bible from end to end and finished. It takes faith
for a man to be paralyzed below the waist and still drag hisself under a car or work a cherry-picker.

Even when his wife scalded him in the bath, he never said a cross word about her. I suppose she
wasn't always my barefoot momma with a cigarette hanging from her lip while she hung out the

clothes. Miami girl, her daddy drank hisself loopy in a bar eating boiled peanuts and watching the
Braves lose. Life ain't been that good for her, but if you make her a good daiquiri once in a while,

and put on that Alan Jackson song she loves, you'll get that smile, that laugh, that way she nods
her head and sucks her teeth, the way old cow pokes do. She first came to Arkansas, on good faith

of a simple life with a workin man, she drove an algae green AMC Hornet, three on the tree, little
rumble in its giddy up. She drove that goatsy sumbitch everywhere. Through talcumed fields, white

flashes of rain, even through her brother's mailbox. She had to brake with both feet and stand on it. None of that power steering and braking. Some days she dips off to the shed just for a little quiet,

a scarf of smoke wreathing her granny-bead neck, sitting on the shop table with her legs up on a sawhorse, watching the shapes of sun through the rust holes. Ain't much more she's ever wanted.

She has faith, the kind that bulldogs you down to Second Baptist when you're tired, when you've lost too much. She crawls in her favorite pew, dreams. Who said dreaming ain't talking to god?

She dreams that hammock in the wind, little panting puppies under all that sunshine. She has it. What sends them Pentecostals dancing through a room full of snakes and sinners. Singing. Faith.

Faith that will bring her one day to a quiet sun-flooded beach she's dreamed of, but never been to.

Everything and everyone here is turning against you

and I remember your lithe hands over me, looking for a way in, but my body was fanged
and scoured to bones and wires. I wish   I could believe in the soul,
                    but it would be just another broken thing in me.
There's so many ways a father can grab a son. And every way you grabbed me marbled my skin.
I remember lightning bugs sparking like matches in a tomb.
                                                I was scattered into summer dark,
sick with the gluttony of pain. I remember my back shoved against the apple tree,
knees squelching in mud, that first time I bristled, dizzy and blind,
piebald shapes coiling in the blackness of my shut eyes, mouth swamped in blood.
Remember my fist, rising. Red clots in the pokeweed.
                                Enough heat in my skull to cook marrow.
I don't remember momma yelling—it was just a horse whinnying.
                        I've carried it quietly a long way, this tattoo with no mark.
I didn't know any better: all my friends were brindled with the mark of their father's belt.

aubade with gut-shot dog

everything's blurry and muted
like the world's wrapped in gauze
daddy's greasy hands shoving the rifle in my chest
I barely hear him say *shoot that god damn dog*
when you see him—don't let him bite you

it's dark out and my dog came back to the yard
padding lighting towards the chicken house
it feels like someone else's arm holding the rifle
tracking the dark figure creeping
through the crackling grasses
lightning bugs tapping on their filaments

I've tried to unmake the memory
tried shattering it to a thousand pieces
but it keeps happening and will never stop happening

I've made headstones for every dog I've lost
paint stirrer crosses dipped in black paint
I've stuck them behind the tree out back
lightning-stuck it keeps growing but crooked
I miss them all of them—the truck-killed
caked into the blue-chip of Crow's Loop
or flung into the ditch to bloat all day long
those that died being too old laying on the porch

pearl strands of foam issue from my dog's mouth
sweat on every inch of my exposed body

I need a clean shot to make it quick
I bite down and squeeze the trigger
but he lunges before I finish
and he's gut-shot and howling

I finish it but I only save him a few minutes of pain
the blade slides through the cotton of his throat
I don't need the spotlight for this

the moon is bright and the night strung together
with strings of bullfrog song and my dog gurgling
the thousands of oblivious stars
the spiderweb of ache in my shoulder
smell of gunpower stitched in my nose and the ringing

my daddy told me I did it right
and slapped me on the back

V

Hunter and He Dog Up a Holler

Tucked in ice, the Pleiades sat shivering in their bundling skins of darkness.
My friend's been dead for a year now, but I still spend my nights on the tailgate,
arching beer cans into to the trash-choked ditch,

                                   hoarfrost sprent across the windshield.

I miss him for the most selfish reasons. I want to get shed of this guilt
that clings to me like sap. I've spent too much time scrubbing my hands.
I wasn't in that field when he left every thought he had smoldering in the summer hay.

Somewhere deep in the vein of the creek bottoms a coyote,

                                 black-tipped and long

is losing himself to the frozen woods, cracking a rabbit's skulk,
gnawing for the last meat, the velvet brain spread lovingly over his teeth.
Third night in a row I'm awake to hear a midnight train

                                   slagging through this sleepy county.

Once when we were kids, he jumped a train and I watched him drift until he was nothing
and he found me two days later when I was fishing—he came to me singing a funny song
but all I can remember of it was:

                    Hunter and he dog up the holler. Look out Mr. Rabbit!

Snow lay in rags along the dark hills like fragments of some lost scripture.
Two stray dogs fighting over a deer heart under a bonecolored moon,

                              the thick cords of their ribs glisten like frosted rebar.

Maybe a trick of the light,   winter's sleight of hand,

                         but I think I see him,

a silver thread lighting through the back acre,

                  so I take a lantern and set out after him.

Tracks: two sets of paws, flecks of blood among clumps of dead jimson.
Boot prints, smell of juniper moonshine, a night grown cankered.

I hear breathing, panting. But when I open the lantern wide I see them:
a joyless choir, a hundred wild hogs, their black eyes swallowing up the lantern light.

Lexicon

Some nights I dream I'm being ripped through a long night, swollen
with gnats, through the summer air strung with spiderwebs

and dew-heavy light, sawbriars and thistle,
through cut hayfields thick with chiggers and sagging barbedwire

fences and pieces of me fell away like little black leaves into beds
of thorns until darkness was general.

I always wake to find the same moonlight glinting in the long grasses out back,
barely enough night left to dream in.

✷

I've been sleeping by the woodstove in a clapboard house
and every morning the ice flowing down the windows like ropes of bear fat
and every morning I poke and jab the scabbed logs back to a lean fire
and my throat is full of horsehair and my nails are broken to slivers and stars
and I can't see the sun for the smoke.

All my memories are gray: gray trees falling through a gray morning of fog,
          gray tattered wings of clouds, gray eyes to see it all.

Sometimes I'm an old hunting dog,
tented hipbones draped in mangy patches of skin,

a scrap of November still on my tongue
                    and sometimes I'm a trembling rabbit in the bramble,
                              my shadow threadbare from running.

✷

Every new year, because even if he didn't know physics,
he still knew today is always smaller than tomorrow,
my grandfather at midnight with a jug of cheap wine stood in the field,
frost sprent and spiraling over every ashen branch, firing his gun at the moon.

And everything for him was black:
                              the black field falling away acre by acre every night,
the barn, sent floating in the winter fields like a nub of ash in a milky globe
and the milky way just an arch of bonemeal on a black sheet.

❋

I've made an altar here to the living crowned in antlers and nightshade
and here I've placed every wrong use of my tongue:

Say winter and mean a plague of starlings sickening the sky black,
say anything about the light feathered with snow,
say south and mean the hunched backs of geese wintering these fields,
say hallelujah but mean hellfire,
say home and mean the crow-haunted barn breaking open.

Say what you want about the flood,
but it's been many years since I seen so many stars

Ruined as I am, I was spun into this life
with a fish bone stuck in my throat—locked
in a soft rain's misgivings. I'm bowfishing
the oldest fields for trapped gars trying to forget
myself to the last scraps of storm-wind
and claw-shaped clouds. Hours are dripping
through my waders. Fifty acres of floodwater
muting even the owls. I can't get shed of Grandmaw—
months on from coming to her reward,
her long nights slashing the bed calico
with strands of sweat, how near the end
all she could do was sleep and beg.
Now she's a filmy coat on the tongue
of Sunday's light. Time makes nothing of us all.
It took some doing to get out here,
where barbedwire hums in the dark
and every creeping thing goes on its belly
through the massive silence. So quiet
I can hear Catawba worms tumbling
in their nests. *Catfish candy*. I cut a line
in the floodwater with my headlamp
chasing a gray bolt through thin grass.
The natural lights have been yanked out
leaving only a ribcage of cloud,
the late coal train muscles down mountains
cut blackly against the far lights of another town.
When I was young and sad, I asked my daddy
what made the whistle at night?
That's river-ghosts singing in the trees.
They ain't here to hurt you none.
I keep moving deeper on posted land,
land even my daddy's never been on,
the sky shakes out more rain.
It's raining in every county in Arkansas.
Everything is alive tonight and lifting
its head blindly, but death sits high
in the cotton wood tree, paring his nails.

Overcup

Riding out the night-clotted backcountry in my father's pickup:
fields sinking into oblivion one more night, porch lights winking out one by one.
This, the sum of all things forgotten or lost out here comes back
through the open window in flustered mess. I think of what it takes to live here;
to sit on the dock on Lake Overcup and watch the night grow thick with mosquitoes,
knowing what you leave is same as what you run to.
It takes a certain kind of person to know what is born of this place:
generations of good tomatoes—blistered globes heavy with seeded blood,
the way the sun strikes the face of Petit Jean Mountain, the glint of a sharp axe blade.
To love the groan and hiss of a clean hammer stroke, the way the nail sinks up in the wood.
Folks out here, the ones that stay, anyhow, they understand that it all means something,
the headstones without names—just dates, every sunk porch like a cracked fist,
it all has to mean something to live on land that has broken better men.

Fishing Report

Bream good on crickets. Crappies for minnows. Clarity: stained.

Trolling down the lake shore, trees strung with blanched bobbers like cotton bolls.

One tree looks like my momma bent over a galvanized tub washing clothes.

It's so easy to become solipsistic out here, caught in god's strung out green iris,

sculling through flooded yards, a lone man sitting on a stump scraping briar

off a saddle with a buck knife. I'm fishing with Buck. He's been sick, always will be.

He says he was born with a hole in his heart. I try to imagine my own heart

and its cotton thud, but all I see in my chest is a shed, plywood and chicken wire,

a dark puddle inside that gets darker and deeper every day. The silence was getting thick,

so I told him about how I prayed to the devil once because god wouldn't answer.

We didn't talk much after that, so I got lost again in the spool of my own thoughts.

Last week I broke open a bale of hay and found a perfect whole cat skull inside.

I gave it to Buck along with a rock out of a drum fish's head. They come in pairs

but I lost the other in the river. Sometimes it's enough. A few hours knocking in the lake.

And the sun breaks open and I feel like a burning quail flushed out of a brush pile.

The Church Essay

Who among you can walk these halls of shattered light, feel the dip and bow of old clapboard, hear
the heat-collapsed notes of the piano railing down I'll Fly Away and not get goose pimples. Church

nights, the woods filling with rib-smoke, huffing out the greasy hinges of Pastor John's homemade
smoker, coal-oil tank. Pastor John, man of the wilderness, his namesake, he hollers down the church

when he stomps and bangs the podium, his silvering mullet shining with sweat and August light.
He loves his flock, but he loves hanging axe heads and felling trees better. The feel of a fluid axe swing,

the hiss of the blade splitting the heart of log. Clean, harsh. He can put an edge so fine on a blade
you could shave a frog's ass. Told me one day *there's things you do for love. For me it's church*,

so he's a preacher man. Only man that could ever keep up with him is Pierre, this old Frenchman
that lives in a half-rotted boathouse in a sleepy riverbend as quiet as a Monday morning church.

He has a diamond blade sharpener he uses to make money, but he was a gourmet chef before
the gout. He ended up in Arkansas somehow or other. Folks talked cause he never went to church.

Chalked it up to European bullshit. Some years back, J.T. Compton wanted a man to climb five pine
trees and paint a stripe near the top for a cutting crew. He offered a hundred dollars to any man

and my daddy bellied up like a hoss to a feed barrel, but got hisself stuck about thirty feet up
and couldn't keep moving. I'll be damned if that hairy little Frenchman didn't climb all them trees

barefoot like a squirrel do. The one time he ever came to church was the big July fourth BBQ.
Everybody was there. Enough meat and booze to drawl every coonskin in the county. Our church

wouldn't fit everybody that came out that evening to that clearing, struck out in the Overcup
darkness between the river and the lake. Horses tremble in the dark. Whistlepigs churn in the dirt.

Twenty pickups lined up by a brush pile burning. From the air it must look like Hell creeping
from up under the earth, but on the ground, it was like living in a lantern rimmed in pine shadows.

They ain't nobody alive that don't remember that night: the booze, dancing, meat right off the smoker.
Rufus holding court: *You can tell when a sweet tater is cooked good. They feel light.*

Old Cloy slumped up against a tree, his boots up on a cooler. He's been in his cup all night
and hollering a end of an old joke: *Mutherstickers, this a fuck up!* Old church ladies cock

a brow his way even if they're on their fourth Bloody Mary. Pastor John is arm wrasslin Peanut
to see who gets the pot likker. *Hit'll make yer pecker harder than a pole barn nail*, says Ella Blue

shining like the jangles on a new tambourine. We are all tucked in the black sheen of an Arkansas night, dark as a black mare's rump, dancing around a bonfire bigger than most folk's home,

Bocephus winding out the speakers. Even the younguns got themselves good and tight, wrassling around in the hay loft, having their first kisses or first fights—either one sacred in this church.

Next morning, we headed off to the jobs waiting to wear us thin, but that night we was many country people set loose, burning it down. I'll be damned if anyone'll tell me that's not a church.

Acknowledgments

Grateful acknowledgement must be made to the following journals in which some of the work in this book has appeared: *The Journal*, *Minnesota Review*, *The Swamp*, *storySouth*, *Gulf Stream*, *Juked*, *Quiditty*, *Copper Nickel*, *KYSO Flash*, *Scalawag*, *Nashville Review*, *Connotation Press*, and *Sou'wester*.

Some poems have appeared in other forms in the chapbook *Hunter and He Dog Up a Holler*, Swamp Editions (2018).

I'm obliged to thank some of the many whose minds have helped bring this book up.

Thanks to my teachers Amy Baldwin, Joey Cole, Sandy Longhorn, Davis McCombs, Judy Jordan, and especially Caroline Lewis, who first started me on this path.

My thanks to the New Harmony Writers Workshop.

Thanks to the many friends, colleagues, and readers of my work who've had a hand in these poems. Some of them are: Cody Smith, Tiana Clark, Laura Ruffino, Anna Knowles, J. Scott Brownlee, Andy Leeming, Zach Harrod, Zac Henderson, and C. Dale Young.

Deep gratitude to Ruth Awad, Brian Barker, and Maurice Manning for reading my work with care and offering kind words and thoughts about it. Their kindness and thoughtfulness is truly amazing.

Thanks to my closest readers Josh Meyers, John McCarthy, and Andrew Hemmert. Thank you for the friendship and for the guidance.

Thanks to myriad happenings and meetings and conversations that have influenced this work.

Finally, my deepest thanks and love and gratitude to my momma, for whom this book is dedicated.

About the Author

James Dunlap is an Arkansas poet and butcher. He studied creative writing at University of Arkansas and Southern Illinois University at Carbondale. His poems have appeared in *Michigan Quarterly Review*, *Nashville Review*, *Copper Nickel*, *The Journal*, and *storySouth*. He is the author of the chapbook *Hunter and He Dog Up a Holler*.